natural disasters
FLOODS

Jil Fine

Children's Press
A Division of Scholastic Inc.
New York / Toronto / London / Auckland / Sydney
Mexico City / New Delhi / Hong Kong
Danbury, Connecticut

Book Design: Erica Clendening
Book Layout: Tahara Anderson
Contributing Editor: Jennifer Silate

Photo Credits: Cover, p. 1 © Chris Graythen/Getty Images; p. 4 courtesy of NASA; p. 6 © Jim Reed/Corbis; p. 10 © Justin Sullivan/Getty Images; p. 13 © Kyle Niemi/ US Coast Guard via Getty; pp. 15, 30 © AP/Wide World Photos; p. 16 © AFP/AFP/ Getty Images; p. 18 courtesy of US Air Force photo by Tech. Sgt. Tracy L. DeMarco; p. 22 © Tariq Mahmood/AFP/Getty Images; p. 24 © Stan Honda/AFP/Getty Images; p. 27 © Bob Mc Millan/FEMA Photo; p. 32 © Ethan Miller/Getty Images; pp. 35, 38 © Robyn Beck/AFP/Getty Images.

Library of Congress Cataloging-in-Publication Data

Fine, Jil.
    Floods / Jil Fine.
    p. cm. - (Natural disasters)
    Includes bibliographical references and index.
    ISBN-10: 0-531-12435-5 (lib. bdg.)   0-531-18721-7 (pbk.)
    ISBN-13: 978-0-531-12435-2 (lib. bdg.)   978-0-531-18721-0 (pbk.)
    1. Floods-Juvenile literature. 2. Hurricane Katrina, 2005-Juvenile
    literature. I. Title. II. Natural disasters (Children's Press)

    GB1399.F52 2007
    551.48'9-dc22

                                                2006008161

CONTENTS

This satellite photo shows Hurricane Katrina as it worked its way over the Gulf Coast in August 2005.

INTRODUCTION

On August 28, 2005, a powerful hurricane named Katrina was churning in the Gulf of Mexico. Hurricane Katrina's winds were more than 160 miles (258 kilometers) per hour. The National Weather Service (NWS) warned that the hurricane could cause widespread devastation. About a million people living in Louisiana, Mississippi, and Alabama fled their homes for safety.

Hurricane Katrina seemed to be headed straight for New Orleans, where more than 460,000 people lived. Many experts believed that the levees, high walls that kept the city safe from flooding, would not be able to stand up under the power of the hurricane. If the levees failed, the waters from the lakes surrounding New Orleans and the Mississippi River would spill into the city. New Orleans was in danger of being destroyed. New Orleans mayor Ray Nagin called for the first-ever total evacuation of the city.

The next morning, Hurricane Katrina hit land. Strong winds blasted the coast. Some gusts were recorded at more than 140 miles (225 km) per hour. Heavy rains caused streams, rivers, and lakes to swell. In New Orleans, the water from surrounding lakes and rivers swept into the city. Winds kicked up waves and sent water flooding over the levees. The water in the streets of New Orleans kept rising. Then several levees broke. Water poured into the city. Homes, businesses, and even lives were destroyed in minutes.

The winds and rain in New Orleans ended on August 29, 2005. The flooding, however, continued for two more days. Water still poured through the broken levees from nearby lakes. Thousands of people were left stranded on the roofs of their homes or on any other high places they could find. About 80 percent of New Orleans was underwater. That mighty flood changed the lives of the people in New Orleans forever.

Floods are one of the most deadly forces in nature. In the following pages, we'll learn more about these dangerous disasters and the flood that swamped New Orleans.

Katrina's powerful winds ripped through New Orleans, tearing down trees and destroying property wherever it went.

A young girl wades along a street in Wisconsin that was flooded by the Mississippi River in 2001.

chapter 1

THE MAKING OF A DISASTER

F loods are one of the most common natural disasters on Earth. In fact, most people in the United States have experienced some sort of flooding. Let's take a closer look at how these deadly disasters are caused and where they usually occur.

RIVER FLOODS

River floods happen quite often. In some areas, rivers overflow every winter or spring. Some people who live in areas where floods are common even build their houses on stilts to protect them from the rising waters! River floods can be created in many different ways.

HEAVY RAINS

Heavy rain is one of the leading causes of floods. Storms can last several minutes or several days. Some storms can drop many inches of water onto an area. When this happens, streams, rivers,

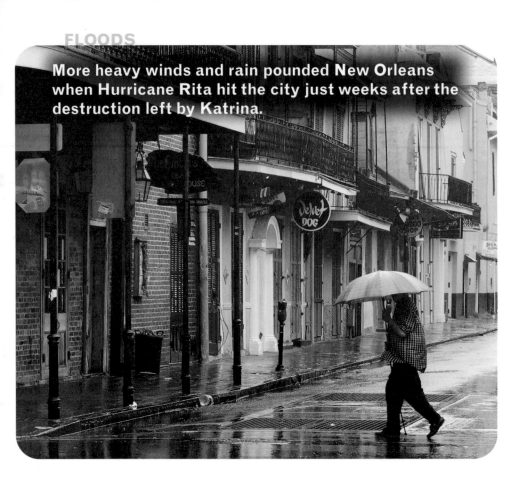

More heavy winds and rain pounded New Orleans when Hurricane Rita hit the city just weeks after the destruction left by Katrina.

lakes, and all other nearby water sources fill. The water has nowhere else to go, so it floods into streets and homes.

Sometimes it is not just one storm that causes a flood. In the spring or winter, a series of powerful thunderstorms can fill streams, rivers, lakes, and reservoirs. Flooding will happen when another storm with heavy rains causes these bodies of water to overflow.

DID YOU KNOW?

Almost half of all natural disasters in the world are floods.

SNOWMELT

Another major cause of flooding is rapid snowmelt. In the winter, it is common for 10–12 inches (25–31 centimeters) or more of snow to build up in northern areas of the United States. If the weather warms suddenly, the snow will melt fast. The water from the melting snow runs into streams and rivers. If the snow melts too fast, the streams and rivers will not be able to handle the extra water.

NO ROOM!

Under normal circumstances, some extra rainwater or water from snowmelt will sink into the ground. The ground acts like a sponge to soak up the water. However, if the ground is already wet the water cannot be absorbed. Very dry or frozen ground will not absorb much water, either. A heavy rain will run off frozen or very dry ground–right into rivers and streams. The rivers and streams can only handle so much water before the excess spills over onto land.

DANGEROUS DEBRIS

The water in rivers and streams sometimes moves very quickly. This fast-moving water can carry tree limbs, trash, and even chunks of ice from frozen parts of the river or stream. This debris can get caught under bridges and block moving water from passing by. Instead, the water flows around the debris. It can flood the bridge and nearby land. When this dam of debris finally moves, the water that was blocked behind it rushes downstream rapidly.

MAN AND THE FLOOD

As the number of people living on Earth grows, so does the need for land. In the last several decades, people around the world have built more houses and businesses near water. These buildings are often put up on land that once absorbed water. The new cities and towns build

Katrina left about 80 percent of New Orleans underwater. The estimated cost of the cleanup is over seven billion dollars.

storm drains to catch water that rolls off the streets after rainfalls. The storm drains take the water to local streams and rivers. Since less water is absorbed by the ground, more water quickly enters drains and then the streams. This quick rise in water causes the streams to flood.

Sometimes the things that people build to stop floods can actually cause them. In some areas where floods are common, people build dams, levees, and other structures to hold back floodwaters. Dams and levees can fail. The water that these structures were built to hold back then rushes onto land. This rush of water can create a deadly situation, just like the one in New Orleans.

COASTAL FLOODS

A coastal flood happens when water from the ocean sweeps onto land. Along ocean coasts, flooding is most often caused by powerful storms, such as tropical storms or hurricanes. Tsunamis can also cause coastal flooding. Hurricanes and tsunamis have caused floods that have affected hundreds of thousands of people in the past several years.

Coastal flooding, shown here in Massachusetts, is often is the result of storm activity.

HURRICANES

Hurricanes are powerful storms that originate over tropical waters. They produce heavy rainfall and strong winds. Both can cause flooding. During a hurricane, winds can push water up onto land. This is called a storm surge. Storm surges have been responsible for major flooding during hurricanes. Hurricanes can cause floods for several miles inland. The storm surge during Hurricane Katrina rose more than 20 feet (6.1 meters) high in several places along the Gulf of Mexico.

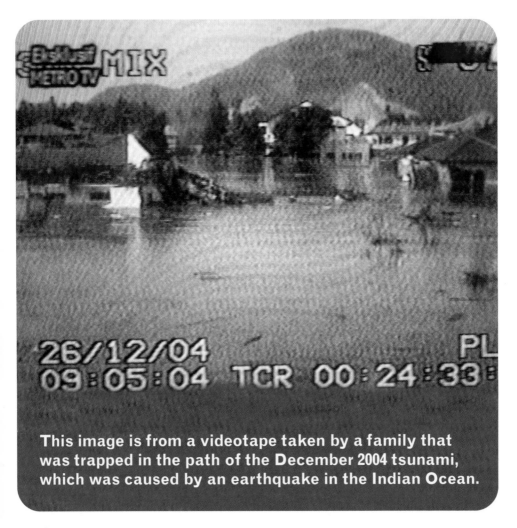

This image is from a videotape taken by a family that was trapped in the path of the December 2004 tsunami, which was caused by an earthquake in the Indian Ocean.

TSUNAMIS

Tsunamis are series of very powerful waves created by an underwater earthquake, a volcanic eruption, or a landslide. A tsunami wave is a large "wall" of water that moves through the ocean with great force. When a tsunami hits, millions of tons of water rush onto land. This causes damaging flooding for areas near the coast. A powerful earthquake under the Indian Ocean caused a devastating tsunami to form in December 2004. Tsunami waves killed hundreds of thousands of people and flooded areas in many different countries.

Floods can be very dangerous no matter where they strike. Sometimes, people only have a few moments to find safety when flooding occurs. It is important that everyone, no matter where they live, knows what to do if a flood threatens.

Many U.S. government workers, such as this Air Force serviceman, monitor floods and weather conditions throughout the country.

chapter 2

PREPARING FOR THE FLOOD

S cientists study floods to find out why and when they happen. They have set up flood centers throughout the United States to watch for floods.

FLOOD WATCH

Streams and rivers across the country are constantly being monitored to tell which ones will flood. Pilots fly over areas that have deep snow to watch for signs of flooding. Scientists also use devices, such as stream gauges, to measure how much streams and rivers swell when different amounts of rain fall over a period of time. There are about seven thousand stream gauges currently in use. The NWS and the United States Geological Survey (USGS) work together to collect the measurements from stream gauges. When a strong storm is forecast, scientists compare the rainfall forecasted with the amount of rain that caused floods in the past. The USGS and NWS warn the public and federal, state, and local agencies of possible floods. These warnings help to save countless lives every year.

FLASH FLOOD

Heavy rains from slow-moving thunderstorms, hurricanes, or tropical storms are the major causes of flash floods, which occur within 6 hours of a rain event. Levee or dam breaks can also cause a flash flood. These floods can destroy buildings and bridges and knock down trees in a matter of minutes. In fact, flash floods cause more deaths than any other weather-related event in the United States.

Flash floods can happen extremely quickly. Many happen at night. Flood centers watch for signs of flash floods and warn people if one is about to happen. Forecasters then issue a flash flood warning or a flash flood watch.

WARNING VS. WATCH

A flash flood watch tells those affected that a flash flood may occur within 6 hours after the rain ends. A flash flood warning indicates that a

DID YOU KNOW?

In 1990, one thunderstorm dumped four inches
(10 cm) of rain on Shadyside, Ohio, in less than
two hours. The flash flood that followed was a
30-foot (9-m) wall of water.

flash flood is happening or will soon happen.
Those who are given a flash flood warning
should seek higher ground immediately.
Floodwaters are very dangerous. It only takes
6 inches (15 cm) of fast-moving water to knock
you off your feet! In New Orleans, there was a
flash flood when the levees broke. The people
there had been warned of possible flooding, but
many were not prepared for the flash flood.

HERE COMES THE FLOOD

Sometimes, floods are long-term events that
can last a week or longer. In this case, a flood
warning or watch is issued when a coastal
flood or river flood threatens an area. This

A Pakistani soldier helps a young boy to safety in Kandar, Pakistan, during a 2005 flood of the Kabul River.

may be because of an approaching heavy thunderstorm or due to fast melting snow. A warning tells of possible flood conditions. A flood watch is called when a flood is occurring or is about to occur. These floods can cause a lot of damage even though they do not happen as fast as flash floods. Floods can destroy cars, homes, and other property. During a flood, wells that supply drinking water may get spoiled with

A DEADLY DRIVE

Many people try to escape floods in their cars. Some even think they can drive through floodwaters to escape. This can be deadly. It only takes 2 feet (61 cm) of water to sweep away most automobiles–even SUVs. About half of the people who die during floods die in their cars.

dirty floodwater. Floods cause billions of dollars of damage every year.

Moving floodwaters can be dangerous. Cars, trees, telephone poles, and even houses can be moved by floodwaters. Many other hazards can be found in floodwaters, too. Power lines that have been pulled down can electrocute people. Toxins in the water can cause illness or disease. During a flood, it is important to listen to the warnings and act quickly if you are asked to leave your home.

Several levees failed to hold back the rising waters caused by Hurricane Katrina. Large parts of New Orleans remained flooded weeks after the disaster.

chapter 3

KATRINA'S FLOOD

As Hurricane Katrina neared land, scientists and officials knew that it was going to cause a lot of damage. Officials warned that it could be the biggest storm to ever hit New Orleans. Many were worried that the city would flood. New Orleans was built 6 feet (1.8 m) below sea level. A system of levees and canals 370 miles (595 km) long kept back the water from the two surrounding lakes and the Mississippi River.

LOOKING AT THE LEVEES

In the months before Katrina, many residents had worried that the levees were leaking. Several people reported flooding in their yards. Engineers who had built the levees said that they would hold up in a hurricane with winds up to 130 miles (209 km) per hour. The day before Katrina hit land, its winds were measured at 175 miles

(282 km) per hour. Forecasters warned that New Orleans could get hit with the worst of the storm.

BRACING FOR KATRINA

As Hurricane Katrina approached, it turned slightly, so New Orleans would not be hit by the most powerful part. Its winds also slowed. It was still very powerful, however. In the hours before Katrina hit land, high winds and rain caused the waters around New Orleans to swell over the levees in some places. When Katrina hit, it was no longer as strong as forecasters had feared. Its winds still howled, though, gusting at times to 140 miles (225 km) per hour.

As the storm moved over New Orleans, the rains increased and the waters rose further. Over time, the pounding waves and the pressure of the rising waters broke through several levees around New Orleans. Floodwaters rushed into the city. Some neighborhoods were covered with 20 feet (6 m) of water. People scrambled to their attics and rooftops. New Orleans may

Homeowners get to work, boarding up the windows of their houses in preparation for the fierce winds and rain of a hurricane.

have dodged the worst of Hurricane Katrina, but it was still in ruins.

S.O.S.

Tens of thousands of people had stayed behind in New Orleans. Many were sick, elderly, or poor. City and federal officials had not been able to get them out of the city before the storm. Many people went to the Superdome football stadium for shelter. Others stayed at home. When the levees broke, water filled 80 percent of New Orleans. Thousands of people were trapped. Flooding had blocked roads, destroyed bridges, and toppled homes. There was no electricity, water, or telephone communication.

The floodwaters did not stop rising after Hurricane Katrina had passed. Important pumps no longer worked. The water from Lake Pontchartrain continued to pour into the city until the water in the lake was no longer higher than the water in the city. People in New Orleans actually saw waves breaking in their streets. Meanwhile, the first attempts to fix the levees failed. The waters continued to rise.

PROTECT OUR PETS

Many shelters in New Orleans and along the Gulf Coast did not allow pets. Thousands of people left their pets at home or in temporary shelters in order to save themselves. After the floods destroyed much of New Orleans, countless numbers of animals were left in the city. Animal rescue organizations across the country joined forces to help them. The Humane Society of the United States estimates that more than 2,200 animals have been reunited with their owners since Katrina.

DANGEROUS WATERS

Fear of drowning was not the only concern for those left behind. Oil, gas, toxic waste, sewage, and other pollutants from damaged pipes and factories were in the floodwaters. People risked serious infections just by entering the water to go for help. In the days after the hurricane, the temperature in New Orleans climbed to 100 degrees Fahrenheit (38 degrees Celsius). Many people were without food, drinking water, or medical help. Federal authorities were unable to get many supplies or workers to the city. Hospitals had to close because they were flooded and had no water or electricity. Many people died because they could not get the medical help they needed. Remaining survivors needed to be rescued from the rising flood before they too became its victims.

DID YOU KNOW?

In a flood, an entire colony of fire ants will form into a ball and float on the water so they do not drown! Large balls of fire ants were seen floating on the floodwaters in New Orleans.

Many residents of New Orleans were rescued from the tops of their homes by helicopters.

These workers, hired by the **U.S. Army Corps of Engineers**, are repairing a flood storm barrier in New Orleans, following the disaster.

chapter 4

AFTER THE FLOOD

The first task facing state and federal officials was to get everyone out of New Orleans. Helicopters and boats went door to door to find survivors and take them to safety. Rescue crews worked around the clock. Thousands of people were saved from the floodwaters.

FIXING THE HOLE

Meanwhile, the Army Corps of Engineers were working to fix the levees in order to pump water out of the city. The engineers used rocks and giant sandbags to plug the holes. Helicopters dropped the 25,000-pound (11,340-kilogram) sandbags onto the levees. It took engineers almost a week to get them all into place. Once this was done, pumps were used to put the floodwater back into the lake.

RECOVERING FROM RITA

Unfortunately, less than one month after Hurricane Katrina, another hurricane approached the area. This storm, Hurricane Rita, sent water crashing into the newly repaired levees. Water once again poured into the streets of New Orleans.

Within a week, though, the water that had just flooded into the city had been pumped out of it. Engineers worked for months to repair the levees. Temporary repairs were finished in January 2006. These repairs would not hold, however, if another hurricane hit New Orleans. In the months to follow, engineers continued the repair work to make the levees strong enough to hold up during the new hurricane season starting in June.

Experts studied the levees and learned that they were not as strong as people had once thought. The experts found that the soil beneath the levees was weak in some places and added to their failure. Changes are being made to make the levees stronger and taller. Experts hope that

The town of Cameron, Louisiana, was in ruins after hurricanes Rita and Katrina.

these changes will protect the people of New Orleans if another storm as big as Katrina hits again. There will also be new pumping stations on the levees. They will be able to pump more water than the old pumps if a flood happens. The large walls of the pumping stations will also help to block a hurricane's storm surge. This construction will take at least another year after the first repairs are finished.

REBUILDING NATURE

Levees and pumps aren't the only way to hold back water. Wetlands also once kept New Orleans safe from many floods. Wetlands are swamps and marshes that are near the coast. In fact, they are vital pieces of the coastal ecosystem. During a hurricane or very strong storm, wetlands act as a speed bump to slow down the rushing water. After many of the levees were built in the 1900s, however, the wetlands around New Orleans started to disappear. The

COSTLY KATRINA

Experts guess that the cost to repair the levees will be about three billion dollars. The total cost of building flood safety structures in New Orleans will probably come to around twenty billion dollars. In total, rebuilding after Hurricane Katrina may cost more than two hundred billion dollars. It is the most costly hurricane in history.

levees not only blocked water from flooding the area, but they kept water from bringing more rich soil to the wetlands. Much of the wetlands in Louisiana are now gone altogether. After Katrina, federal agencies and others realized they must work to bring the wetlands back in order to reduce the amount of flooding in New Orleans in years to come.

WHERE TO REBUILD?

In the months following Katrina, officials and people who had lived in New Orleans argued over where to rebuild. Many officials did not want to rebuild where the floods had been the worst. They feared more flooding. Many people, however, wanted to return to where their homes had once been. The city had to make some tough decisions about where to build. Six months after the hurricane, city officials and residents were still trying to come to an agreement.

COMING HOME

People slowly returned to the city where they could. About one-quarter of the people who

The school these students went to was destroyed by Katrina. In this photo, they say the Pledge of Allegiance in their new, temporary school.

had lived in New Orleans before Katrina were able to return to the city three months later. The rest were still living in shelters and other people's homes across the country. New jobs were created as rebuilding began, but there were not enough homes for all the workers. Many people had to leave the city after work each night.

In time, New Orleans will be rebuilt. The levees will be higher and stronger than they ever were. Homes and businesses will return, though not as many as before. The flooding during Katrina changed the city and the people who lived there forever. New Orleans may never be the city it once was, but it will be better prepared for the next natural disaster.

HISTORY'S EIGHT DEADLIEST
FLOODS

⑦⑧
Europe

North
America

Atlantic
Ocean

Africa

South
America

❶ Yellow River, China
1931 1,000,000-3,700,000 deaths

❷ Yellow River, China
1887 900,000-2,000,000 deaths

❺ Ru River, Banqiao Dam, China
1975 230,000 deaths

❻ Yangtze River, China
1931 145,000 deaths

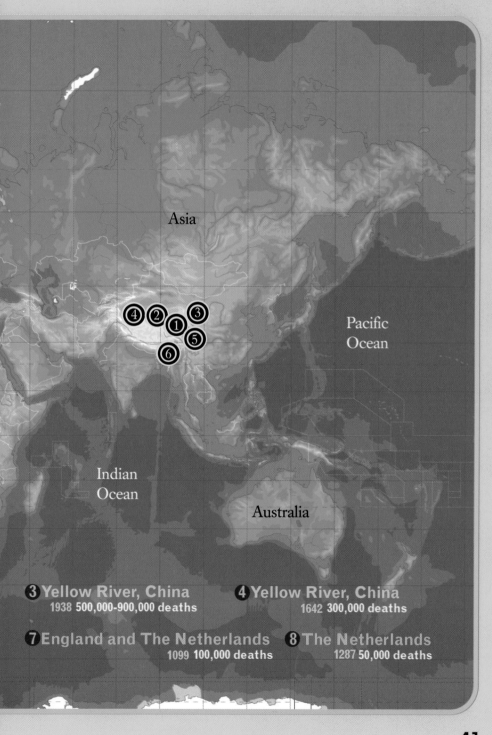

Asia

Pacific
Ocean

④②①③
⑤
⑥

Indian
Ocean

Australia

❸Yellow River, China
1938 **500,000-900,000 deaths**

❹Yellow River, China
1642 **300,000 deaths**

❼England and The Netherlands
1099 **100,000 deaths**

❽The Netherlands
1287 **50,000 deaths**

NEW WORDS

absorb (ab-**zorb**) to soak up liquid

coastal flood (**kohst**-uhl **fluhd**) water from the sea overflowing its normal limits; usually caused by powerful storms

dams (**damz**) strong barriers built across streams or rivers to hold back water

debris (duh-**bree**) scattered pieces of something that has been broken or destroyed

devastation (**dev**-uh-stay-shuhn) terrible damage or destruction

earthquake (**urth**-kwayk) a sudden, violent shaking of Earth, caused by a shifting of its crust

electrocute (i-**lek**-truh-kyoot) to injure or kill with a severe electric shock

evacuation (i-**vak**-yoo-ay-shuhn) moving people away from an area because of danger

hurricane (**hur**-uh-kane) a violent storm with high winds that starts in the tropical regions of the Atlantic Ocean or the Caribbean Sea and then travels north, northeast, or northwest

NEW WORDS

landslide (**land**-slide) a sudden slide of earth and rocks down the side of a mountain or a hill

levees (**lev**-eez) banks built up near a river to prevent flooding

river floods (**riv**-ur **fluhdz**) floods that are caused by heavy rain, water from melted snow, or dams or debris in rivers

storm surge (**storm surj**) a rise in water level on shore created by hurricane-force winds over open water

stream gauges (**streem gayj**-ez) devices used to watch the level of water in streams

swell (**swel**) to grow larger, greater, or stronger

tsunamis (tsoo-**nah**-meez) very large, destructive waves caused by underwater earthquakes or volcanic eruptions

volcano (vol-**kay**-noh) a mountain with vents through which lava (hot, liquid rock), ash, cinders, and gas erupt, sometimes violently

wetlands (**wet**-landz) land where there is much moisture in the soil

FOR FURTHER READING

Allan, Tony. *Wild Water: Floods.* Chicago: Raintree Publishers, 2005.

Ceban, Bonnie, J. *Floods and Mudslides: Disaster and Survival.* Berkeley Heights, NJ: Enslow Publishers, 2005.

Duden, Jane. *Floods! Rising, Raging Waters.* Leawood, KS: Perfection Learning, 1999.

Eagen, Rachel. *Flood and Monsoon Alert!* New York: Crabtree Publishing Co., 2004.

Lauber, Patricia. *Flood.* Washington, D.C.: National Geographic Children's Books, 1996.

ORGANIZATIONS

National Weather Service
1325 East West Highway
Silver Spring, MD 20910
http://www.nws.noaa.gov/

United States Geological Survey
12201 Sunrise Valley Drive
Reston, VA 20192
Phone: (703) 648-4000
http://www.usgs.gov/

RESOURCES

WEB SITES

FEMA for Kids: Floods
http://fema.gov/kids/floods.htm
The Federal Emergency Management
Association (FEMA) has tons of information
about where floods happen, how to stay safe
in a flood, and more on their Web site.

PBS: InFocus: Floods
http://www.pbs.org/newshour/infocus/
floods.html
Learn about floods and read first-person
accounts of flood survivors on this informative
Web site.

Weather Wiz Kids: Rain and Floods
http://www.weatherwizkids.com/Rain.htm
This Web site has a lot of information about
rain and flood watches and warnings.

INDEX

INDEX

ABOUT THE AUTHOR

Jil Fine has written more than one hundred titles for children. She is a member of the Society of Children's Book Writers and Illustrators.